S is for Story

A Writer's Alphabet

Written by Esther Hershenhorn and Illustrated by Zachary Pullen

Sleeping Bear Press‎
310 North Main Street, Suite 300
Chelsea, MI 48118
www.sleepingbearpress.com

© 2009 Sleeping Bear Press is an imprint of Gale, a part of Cengage Learning.

Printed and bound in China.

First Edition

10 9 8 7 6 5 4 3 2 1

Library of Congress Cataloging-in-Publication Data

Hershenhorn, Esther.
S is for story : a writer's alphabet / written by Esther Hershenhorn;
illustrated by Zachary Pullen.
p. cm.
ISBN 978-1-58536-439-8
1. Authorship—Juvenile literature. 2. Alphabet books—Juvenile literature.
I. Pullen, Zachary, ill. II. Title.
PN159.H47 2009
808.3—dc22
2009005433

To the talented writers (and readers too, of course!)
of Chicago's Louisa May Alcott School.

With special thanks to Ms. Michelle Knight and
Miss Jenny Vincent's '08 Fifth Graders.

ESTHER

For the letter H and the letter R,
two of my favorites.

ZAK

A is for the Alphabet
our letters six plus twenty,
that build the words,
that build the tales,
we read and write aplenty.

People have been *telling* tales forever. But how they came to write those tales for others to read is a whole different story.

At first, people drew pictures of their ideas and words on cave walls or carved tiny symbol-like wedges into clay tablets they baked. The ancient Egyptians drew tiny pictures they named *glyphs* to represent their words. Eventually, the Phoenicians created a writing system of ordered letters, each letter representing a single sound or syllable. Combining the syllables allowed people to create a limitless number of words.

The Greeks adopted this system, added vowels and named it *alphabetos*, after the first two letters, *alpha* and *beta*. The Romans spent several centuries tweaking the system, creating the Latin alphabet English-speaking people use today.

Recognizing letters and the sounds they make is the first step to learning how to read and write. Alphabet books, songs, soup, and even jump-rope jingles teach us all our ABCs.

"Begin at the beginning and go on till you come to the end: then stop."
—Lewis Carroll, *Alice's Adventures in Wonderland*

B b

B must be for Book, of course,
cover-wrapped bound pages,
a treasure chest
of gold and gems,
prized bounty for all ages.

Just as someone had to invent the alphabet, someone had to invent the book. Wood and paper replaced the Egyptians' clay; the Romans' bound, covered sheets of paper known as *codices* replaced tablets and scrolls. Johannes Gutenberg's invention of moveable type allowed books to be more easily printed and published. The word *publish* truly means "to print and give to the public, or people."

No matter how we produce and store books today, traditionally, electronically, or via the latest technology, books offer anything and everything to anyone and everyone—from maps, recipes, stories, and songs to paintings, poems, puzzles, and facts.

Here's a trick: read like a writer. Once you've read a story as a reader, return to the pages wearing your WRITER's cap. Notice how the author kept you turning the pages.

Here's another trick: read about *other* writers. A *biography* is a written account of a person's life. Read how contemporary or long-ago writers gathered their ideas and learned and honed their craft.

"I don't know a single writer who wasn't a reader first."

—Andrew Clements

C is for the Character,
every story's star,
the one for whom
we cheer, we care,
with whom we travel far.

Most stories tell of a character, a particular someone—human or not, real or imagined, who claims the page like a movie star claims the screen.

It's that character who pulls us in and keeps us reading. We travel along, living the story.

Think of Alice, Peter Pan, or Kate DiCamillo's Despereaux. Think of your favorite character from your favorite book.

While many elements such as setting and plot shape a story, character plays an especially important role. Character sets the story in motion.

The writer's job is to create round, not flat, characters. Knowing *each* story character from the inside out helps you do just that.

Imagine your characters' Birthday Wishes, to learn their needs and wants, or their deepest, darkest secrets, to learn their fears and obstacles.

Interview your characters, asking important questions. Their answers will tell you their thoughts and actions.

Immerse yourself in your characters' lives, especially before their stories begin.

"What happens is a reciprocal gift between writer and reader: one heart in hiding reaching out to another."
—Katherine Paterson

C c

A *first* draft is a beginning. The writer writes, telling himself the story. Word choice, spelling, and punctuation matter little. Many writers underline words and sentences they know require attention, returning to them in a later draft.

The need for drafts proves most writing is *re*-writing. Once *you* know your story, subsequent drafts offer you opportunities to tell that story the best way possible to your readers.

Or, listeners, as in the case of Abraham Lincoln. Numerous myths surround the president's writing of his 272-word Gettysburg Address. Lincoln first wrote his words on White House stationery, thinking about his speech's theme. Over seventeen days he revised, sometimes on envelopes. Some say he even used the top of his stovepipe hat as a writing surface while riding the train to Gettysburg. Once there, he continued to revise up until his next day's delivery.

Few of Lincoln's many drafts remain, reminding writers: save your writing!

"I start like most writers start—with a very bad first draft which becomes something to fix, and change, and hopefully make better."

—Pam Muñoz Ryan

D d

So, **D**? It's for the Drafts we write,
from rough to finally ready,
our chance to tell our good tale well,
rewriting,
slow and steady

When it's time to ready your work for presentation, replace your WRITER'S cap with an EDITOR's visor. Look at your work carefully. Focus first on the story or content. Do the beginning, middle, and end come together logically? Did you deliver the story you promised?

Next focus on how you told your story. Did you tell your story in scenes, with characters speaking their words as dialogue?

Editing your final draft is like polishing a precious stone. Check for flaws in spelling, punctuation, capitalization, and grammar.

If you need help, turn to a reference book. Author E. B. White's book on how to correctly use English sits on many writers' desks. "Remember," he wrote, "the heart of your sentence beats in strong verbs, concrete nouns, and vivid descriptions!"

☛ **A Writer's Tip:** put your work away for a day or a week before you edit, making sure you reread from a printed copy.

Then E? It's for the page we Edit,
making sure all's right:
no misspelled names,
   no missing marks,
   no unclear words in sight.

E e

Ff

F is for spun Fairy Tales,
raising tears and laughter,
from "Once upon a time…"
until…
the "…happily ever after."

Fairy tales are one example of the simple tales folks told and still tell all around the world. Often, the stories' humans confront witches, wizards, and dragons, both good and bad; and usually, some kind of magic eventually wipes away sadness and evil.

Frenchman Charles Perrault was one of the first to collect and print fairy tales. His 1697 volume included "Red Riding-Hood." One century later, the brothers Jacob and Wilhelm Grimm gathered German folktales. Originally published for adults, their *Grimm's Fairy Tales* collection offered "Little Red-Cap," a version of "Red Riding-Hood."

Many consider Danish poet and writer Hans Christian Andersen the Father of the Modern Fairy Tale. Several of Andersen's original tales reflected his sad childhood. He'd longed for love, like the Little Mermaid; he'd lived as an outsider, like the Ugly Duckling.

In 1900, L. Frank Baum wrote America's first fairy tale, the fantasy *The Wonderful Wizard of Oz*.

"Fairy tales are more than true: not because they tell us that dragons exist, but because they tell us that dragons can be beaten."

—G.K. Chesterton

Writers and readers classify stories by kind or genre, pronounced *zhan-ruh*. Each category has its own structure and set of rules. Genre choices for fiction include folktales, fantasy, and science fiction. Genre choices for nonfiction include essays, memoirs, and autobiographies.

Most Fantasy has its roots in folktales. Welsh myths inspired several of author Lloyd Alexander's fantasies, while King Arthur legends sparked a Susan Cooper series. A fantasy features an ordinary character in an imagined world so believable the reader is willing to travel along. As in realistic fiction, the character must solve his problem on his own; however, the solution sheds light on important truths.

The everyday characters of Science Fiction must also solve their own problems, although this genre offers plausible events and worlds that *might* exist, someday, some-where. In Robert C. O'Brien's novel *Mrs. Frisby and the Rats of NIMH*, a widowed mouse seeks help from rats once the object of scientific experiments.

Writers often combine genres in telling a story. In the *Bunnicula* chapter book series, James Howe mixes an animal fantasy with a mystery.

G

g

G begins the French word Genre,
a way to group stories by kind.
History, Mystery,
Folktale, Myth.
Each boasts rules to mind.

H h

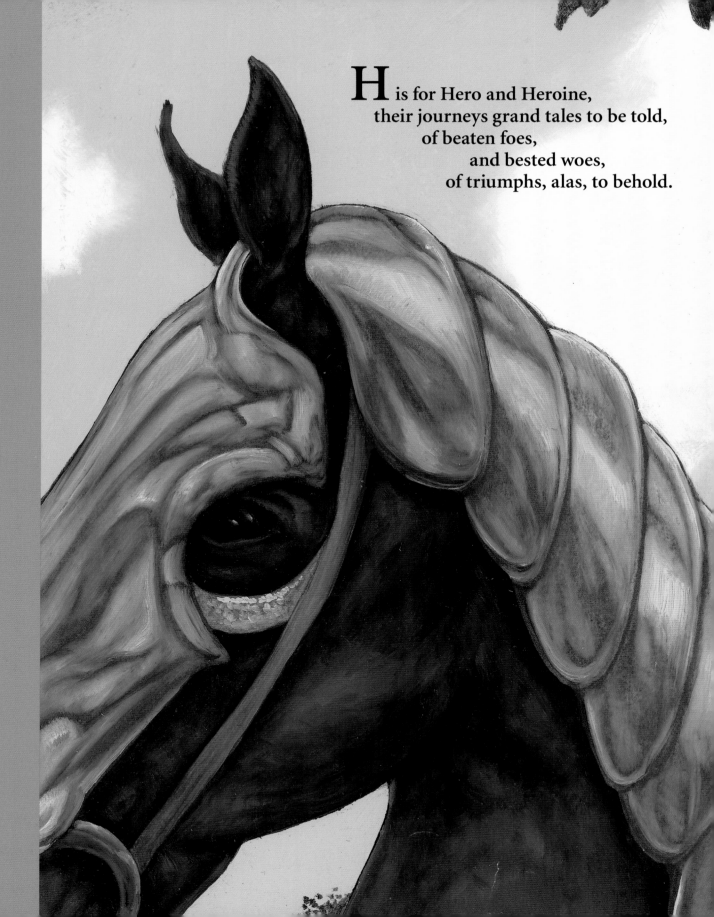

H is for Hero and Heroine,
their journeys grand tales to be told,
of beaten foes,
and bested woes,
of triumphs, alas, to behold.

Hurrah for our Heroes and Heroines!
They journey forth, flawed and ordinary,
meeting friends and foes, digging deep
within, surmounting all obstacles to return
triumphant.

The Greek god Hercules had twelve
tasks to complete in order to achieve his
Hero status. One such labor? To slay a
lion no weapon could kill!

A lightning-shaped forehead scar marks
the much-loved Hero Harry Potter. From
the beginning of Book One in J.K. Rowling's
fantasy, through and to the end of Book
Seven, Harry struggles to defeat evil. Yet
emerging a young man, he understands
love and loss, right and wrong.

Kansas-born Heroine Dorothy Gale
journeys through Oz, seeking a way home.
Throughout L. Frank Baum's fairy tale,
Dorothy and her friends continue to strug-
gle—against flying monkeys, an evil witch,
a bumbling wizard, until at last she sees
where her own power lies.

A Writer's Tip: take heart from
your Heroes and Heroines if writing
becomes difficult.

"Mice are my heroes because, like
children, mice are little and have to learn
to be courageous and use their wits."
—Brian Jacques

Ii

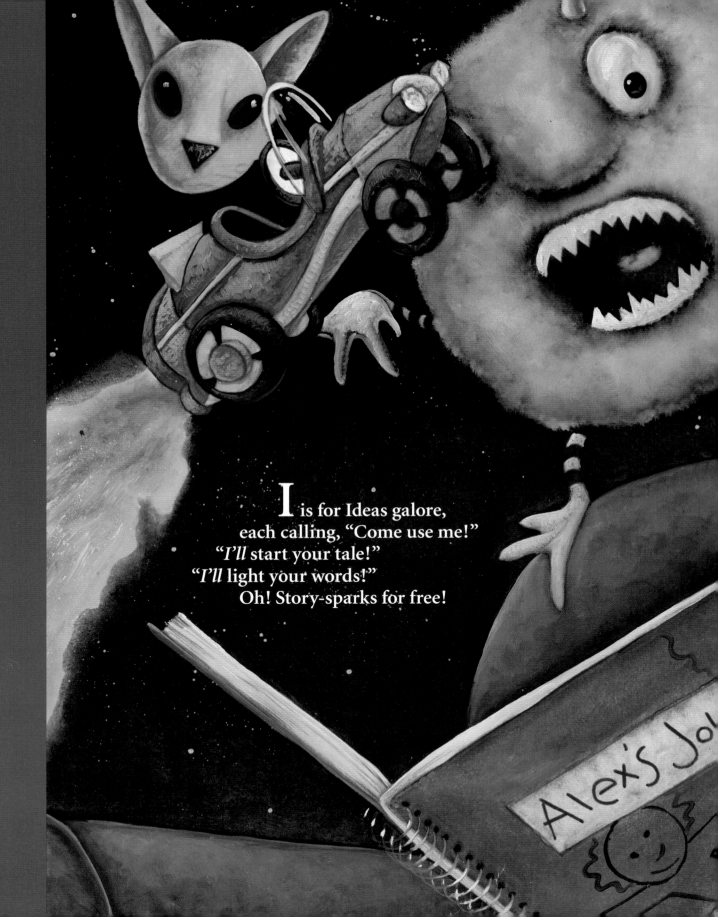

Good news! Ideas live anywhere and everywhere. The "red walls" of Brian Jacques' childhood neighborhood sparked his fantasy series. The idea for Linda Sue Park's novel *A Single Shard* about a long-ago Korean potter appeared in a history book she'd read to research other stories.

Even better news: anytime's a good time to catch an idea. Jacqueline Woodson's wonderings about Conduit Avenue while driving to and from a New York City airport led to her novel *Feathers*.

The best news of all? Any idea *could become* a story. A story idea is neither "good" nor "bad."

Brainstorming lets you see an idea's story possibilities. Try free writing: begin with the idea as it first appeared, but as your mind changes direction, follow each new thought. Or write down your idea as a topic or title, then list, cluster, or web the words and thoughts that come to mind naturally.

Once a story possibility strikes your fancy, spend time imagining. Wonder, suppose, ask, "What if?"

↠ **A Writer's Tip:** create a special box, journal, or computer file to hold your story ideas.

I is for Ideas galore,
each calling, "Come use me!"
"*I'll* start your tale!"
"*I'll* light your words!"
Oh! Story-sparks for free!

Louisa May Alcott. Lewis and Clark. Henry David Thoreau. Each kept a journal and so can you.

A journal is a notebook for recording what happens in your life and your reactions to those events. You choose your writing time, theme, style, readers. Be sure to note each entry's date and setting. Revisiting your journal lets you re-explore your life.

Louisa May Alcott chronicled her childhood, Lewis and Clark their trip west in 1803, Henry David Thoreau his life at Walden Pond.

A diary is a notebook too, but for recording daily personal thoughts and happenings you want to keep private. Anne Frank began her famous diary in 1942, unaware her early death would make her words public.

Today's *blogs*, or Web logs, are another kind of journal, an online version that invites readers to interact with the author.

➣ **A Writer's Tip:** visit author Web sites to read their blogs and journals.

"When I open my journal, it feels like I'm a child going into my room and closing the door."

—Jacqueline Woodson

J is for your Journal,
yours alone to write,
a record true
of what you do,
morning, noon, or night.

Jj

K is for four Kinds of Writing,
each a style to know.
Describe or preach?
Recount or teach?
Think purpose, then readers, then GO!

Descriptive

Expository

Narrative

Persuasive

K K k k

Writing styles vary. So how can you choose the best style for telling your story?

Think first about your purpose. Think next about your readers. Then carefully choose, order, and arrange your words to fit the four most common kinds of writing.

Descriptive writing *describes*. Words paint a picture, showing the reader someone, something, someplace. Specific and sensory details help focus and brighten the image.

Persuasive writing persuades or *convinces* someone to change his opinion. Selected details support a particular viewpoint. Think political speeches, religious preaching, and newspaper editorials.

Narrative writing *narrates* or recounts the story of something that happened to someone, sometime, somewhere. Sequenced scenes order the events from the beginning to the end.

Expository writing *informs* or teaches, exposing the reader to new subjects or thoughts. Thoughtful organization of the necessary facts and information increases clarity and guarantees understanding. Think school reports, biographies, and newspaper accounts.

"Whenever I write.....I'm always trying to use combinations of words and ways of telling the story that are unique to me."
—Kathleen Krull

L is for Letters,
text-ed, typed, or penned.
We thank or ask,
confess, request,
then stamp, post, or click SEND.

Fan letters. Form letters. Chain letters. Santa letters. Love letters. Pen Pal letters. Oh, the opportunities!

A letter, whether friendly or business, includes a date, greeting, appropriate sign-off, and signature. The letter-writer considers the letter's purpose and recipient.

Beatrix Potter was a prolific letter-writer. In fact, *The Tale of Peter Rabbit* began as a Get Well letter to a friend's son. "I don't know what to write to you," she penned, "so I shall tell you a story about four little rabbits..."

Many authors' characters tell their stories in letter form. In Beverly Cleary's *Dear Mr. Henshaw*, Leigh Botts' author fan letters eventually become journal entries. Leigh signs one letter "De Liver De Letter De Sooner De Better."

E-mails and text messages use letter shorthand too. Had Leigh been text-ing Mr. Henshaw, he could have written "TSTB"—"the sooner the better." A text message usually contains about one hundred and sixty characters. To shorten messages, writers delete vowels, the very letters the Greeks added to create our alphabet.

•❖ **A Writer's Tip:** match your writing style to your letter's purpose.

L1

M m

M? Ah, M's for Magic!
Writing's simply that!
What if?, suppose,
stir words you chose,
pull stories from your hat!

If only stories appeared as magically as Mary Poppins did, blown in by a changing wind.

Yet writing *is* magic.

Snatch an idea, imagine its possibilities, shape it, reshape it, creating characters, plotlines, scenes, and resolutions; write, rewrite, edit, submit, resubmit, publish, connect with readers. A story lives where once there had been nothing. Presto! Abracadabra! Chango! Voilá!

No one knows both writing and magic better than Newbery medalist Sid Fleischman, author of *The Whipping Boy* and *The Story of the Great Houdini*, who practiced sleight of hand long before he wrote his humorous tall tales, cleverly-plotted adventures and biographies. Fleischman first learned how to make handkerchiefs vanish by reading books at his local library. He published his first book, a collection of paper match sticks, at age 19. Seeing his name in print changed his life's direction. Once again, Fleischman returned to his library, this time to learn a new craft, writing.

"We are all looking for magic......But indeed we have to wave the wand for ourself."
—P. L. Travers

A Writer's Notebook *isn't* a journal and it *isn't* a diary. Author Ralph Fletcher describes it as a place for anyone to live like a writer, anytime, anywhere.

Use your Writer's Notebook to describe a feeling, brainstorm an idea, or write that joke you've been thinking about. Play with poetry and words, list interesting names you've heard, or write a letter to your story character's worst enemy. Observe, note, respond, react, play, polish, create, experiment. The only rule? Always have your Writer's Notebook handy, whether it's a paper notebook or a file on your computer.

Many writers use their Writer's Notebooks to keep track of a writing project, noting research, rough drafts, loose ideas, and schedules.

Several children's books feature notebook-carrying characters. For instance, in *Harriet the Spy*, sixth-grader Harriet M. Welsch writes down everything she sees in a secret notebook, determined to become an author some day.

⚮ A Writer's Tip: copy words, sentences, or poems you admire into your Writer's Notebook, to reread, study, savor, and model.

So **N**? It's for Notebook,
a writer's must for sure,
for catching, keeping,
any time,
thoughts, ideas, and more.

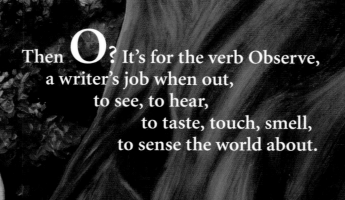

Then **O**? It's for the verb Observe,
a writer's job when out,
to see, to hear,
to taste, touch, smell,
to sense the world about.

O o

Your writer's job is to pay attention to the world around you.

Use your five senses to see, hear, taste, touch, and smell. Raise your writer's antennae to notice and discover, to become aware.

Be sure to note your observations in your Writer's Notebook. One might spark a story. Watching how her cats and dogs talked to one another inspired Sheila Burnford to write *The Incredible Journey*. Another *Ah-ha!* observation might find its way into a poem. Poet Lee Bennett Hopkins says, "Good poems make us say, 'Yes, that's just how it is!'"

Observations become sensory details, giving your reader that "You are there!" feeling: the musty smell of an abandoned room, the hush of a crowd, a wool sock's scratch and itch.

A keen observer from childhood on, President Theodore Roosevelt charged through his days, living life to the fullest. His observations filled nature notebooks, travel journals and personal diaries, over 150,000 letters, and twenty books.

"The world, under the microscope of your attention, opens up like a beautiful, strange flower....."

—Kate DiCamillo

Pcan only be for Plot,
characters in action!—
rising, falling,
try-by-try,
craving satisfaction.

Plot is your main character's plan of action to get the something he needs or wants. The actions shape or structure your story, creating a beginning, middle, and end.

At the start, obstacles complicate your character's actions. Your plot's middle is a muddle, the situation worsening as your character acts and *re*-acts. Both your character and reader ask, "What happens next?!" The story rises to its highest point, the climax. Yet, alas, your character, changed and grown, knows what must be done. The "OH, NO!" moment becomes an "Oh, yes!" The story's end or resolution satisfies all.

Your characters must act as they truly are. Some writers know their characters' actions instantly; others discover them as they write and revise.

Once you're ready to tell your story to your reader, summarize your story's plot in one sentence to stay focused on your characters' actions. Do you recognize this summary? "Willy Wonka's famous chocolate factory is opening at last! But only five lucky children will be allowed inside."

"If everything goes smoothly, it's not a story!"

—Linda Sue Park

P p

The Question Words—*who, what, when, where, how,* and *why*—come in handy when you're growing a story. Their answers shine a light on your story's parts.

Ask *Who?* to determine your story's characters.

Ask *What?* to determine your characters' needs and problem.

Ask *When?* to learn the time your story takes place.

Ask *Where?* to learn your story's setting.

Answering *How?* shows your story's plot, the characters' actions and re-actions from beginning to end.

Answering *Why?* lets you peek inside your characters' hearts, to learn their wants, needs, and fears.

Give yourself time to answer each question. Sometimes one or two answers are enough to start your story. Knowing only a place and a time in her grandmother's life sparked Pam Muñoz Ryan's novel *Esperanza Rising.*

Of course, change one answer and *abracadabra!*: a new story appears! Fractured Fairy Tales set a familiar story in a different time or setting, or in the case of Jon Scieszka's storybook *The True Story of the Three Little Pigs,* replace the Hero with the Villain.

Q is for the Question Words,
Ask *Who? What? When?* and *Where?*
next *How?*, then *Why?*
and by-and-by,
you'll have a tale to share.

R r

R is for Revision.
You see your draft anew.
A second chance,
to make tales dance.
Lucky, lucky you!

Revision is an opportunity to see or *vision* your words *again*, to once more look at your earlier drafts with new and fresh eyes.

Novelist Judy Blume uses her first draft to discover her story's puzzle pieces, the second draft to understand those pieces, the third to paint a picture using those pieces.

A successful revision requires time and patience.

Dr. Seuss's *The Cat in the Hat* began as a challenge from his publisher to use up to 250 words from a list of 300 to 400 words to write a reading primer children would not be able to put down. Dr. Seuss figured "he could knock it off in a week or so." The book's numerous revisions took a year and a half.

E.B. White labored several years writing *Charlotte's Web*. It wasn't until his eighth draft that he chose the novel's opening line, "Where's Papa going with that axe?"

"The beautiful part of writing is that you don't have to get it right the first time, unlike, say, a brain surgeon."
—Robert Cormier

S is for Story,
so brilliant in its might,
to help us see
    ourselves, our world,
        in, oh, such dazzling light.

Story has both power and brilliance, no matter the telling, recited, sung, or seen. A story's words illuminate what matters, for the teller and the listener, for the writer *and* the reader.

Henry Wadsworth Longfellow's famous ballad recounts the night a patriot rode horseback through Concord's streets to warn citizens the British were coming. Children still listen to hear of the midnight ride of Paul Revere.

The sight of the star-spangled American flag waving in the dawn's early light after a War of 1812 battle inspired Francis Scott Key to pen a poem. The words first appeared in printed handbills. Later someone set the words to an English melody. In 1931 Congress declared Key's poem our national anthem.

Comic strips let people see stories graphically presented in sequenced panels.

In 1895 Richard Outcault created the first cartoon that let characters speak, in bubbles drawn above their heads. Superman, the first Actions Comic hero, appeared in 1938. Today's manga and graphic novels are variations of this form.

"....re-telling is the way we humans try to make sense of things."

—Lois Lowry

S
S

T stands for Tall Tales,
stories grand and bold,
of lumberjacks,
their pals and gals,
of railroad men of old.

Folks have been telling Tall Tales forever. Their larger-than-life Heroes and Heroines make memorable characters.

A Tall Tale's trademarks are easy to spot: exaggeration, humorous exploits or human tragedy, and imaginative language. Figures of speech, such as similes, metaphors, and hyperboles, help this genre shine.

A simile is usually introduced by the words *like* or *as* and compares and contrasts two things that are generally not alike. For example, some folks say that when the legendary lumberjack Paul Bunyan swung his axe in the Northwest woods, those big trees fell like toothpicks.

A metaphor also compares or contrasts two unlikely things but doesn't use the words *like* and *as*. For instance, in telling the railroad tale of American steel-driver John Henry's battle against the steam-powered drill, one storyteller said Big Bend Mountain was "a heap of hard anger and hurt feelings."

Hyperboles are exaggerated similes and metaphors. As in, Tall Tale giant Dona Flor made tortillas so large, the children of her Southwest pueblo village used them as rafts.

Becoming a writer is easy. Simply place the suffix *er*, which means "a person who," after the verb *write*.

But succeeding as a writer demands hard work. A writer must finish what he starts, polish his words, put forth his best, no matter the challenges.

Author Karen Hesse never gave up on herself or her childhood writer's dream, shaped by her fifth grade teacher's belief she was "good with words." She worked as a waitress, nanny, librarian, personnel officer, farm laborer, substitute teacher, and book reviewer, all the while writing poems, stories, and books.

After high school, novelist Christopher Paul Curtis worked ten-hour days on an automobile assembly line, writing on thirty-minute breaks he arranged with his door-hanging partner. A later college manuscript became the novel *The Watsons Go to Birmingham* which eventually lost out in a publishing contest. But he did win an editor plus the chance to revise, allowing the book to go on to win a Newbery Honor.

"Never fear failure. Embrace it. It's the only sure path to success."
—J. Patrick Lewis

U is for Unstoppable,
Your writer's cry? "Go! Go!"
Write-write full steam.
Work hard. Still dream.
Bounce back. Succeed. Then glow.

V v

V? Why, V must be for Voice,
 our written words that speak,
of who we are,
what makes us *us*,
 what makes us each unique.

Each of us has a speaking voice, even when we write. We live on the page, somewhere in between the lines. Our readers hear us, loud and clear, when we care about our stories, write from our hearts, and choose and order words as only we can.

To make sure *your* voice comes across, write as if you're telling your story to a friend. Lean over while you write, imagining you're whispering in someone's ear. Or write your story in a letter, as Beatrix Potter did, or in an urgent e-mail, as Paula Danziger and Ann Martin did in their series *Snail Mail No More*.

Of course, the characters in the story you're telling speak too, each with a unique voice. Corresponding with your characters helps you hear their speech patterns and word choice. One might stammer; another might phrase each sentence as if posing a question.

➥ A Writer's Tip: ask yourself and your characters, "Why is it important the world know your story?"

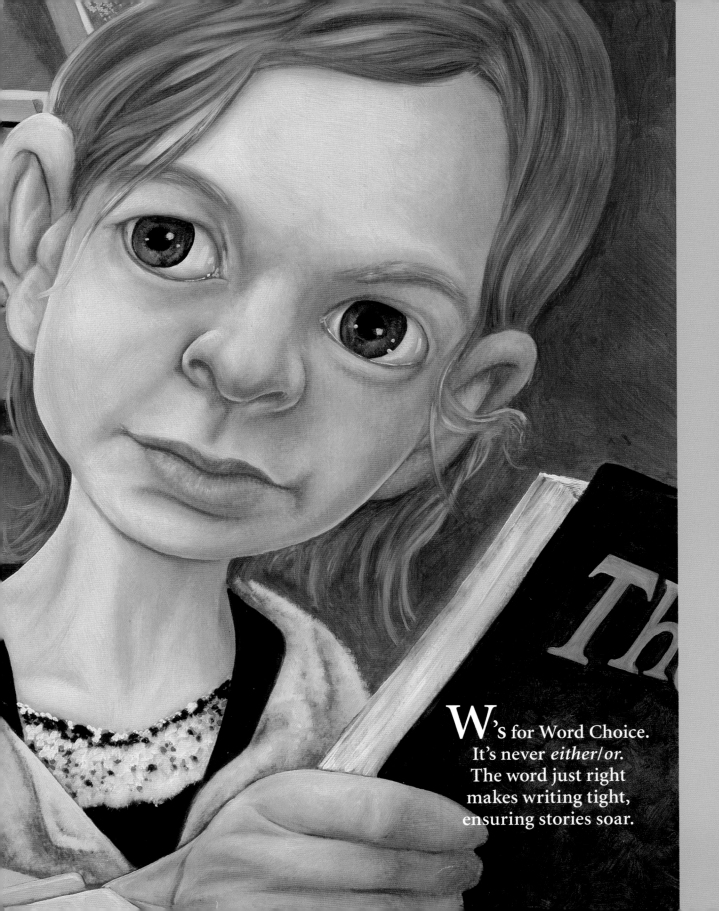

W's for Word Choice.
It's never *either/or*.
The word just right
makes writing tight,
ensuring stories soar.

Writers build stories, word by word, sentence by sentence. Skillful writers choose their words carefully.

Does your character *walk* or *shuffle*, *stroll* or *strut*? Is the day *hot* or *humid* or *suffocating*? Think what you want your reader to sense and know. Specific words create specific images.

Use a thesaurus, or dictionary of synonyms, to find the word that best suits your character, action, scene, or voice. And pay close attention to the verbs you choose. The correct verb not only saves you words, it drives your sentence.

Choosing characters' names also demands careful thought. In *Gossamer*, Lois Lowry named her nonhuman dream-givers Littlest and Thin Elderly. J. K. Rowling imagined Albus wandering about, humming, so she gave the Headmaster the last name of "Dumbledore," an old English word for "bumblebees."

➤ **A Writer's Tip:** if you set your story in another time, read books and newspapers from that period to find words and names people used.

"The difference between the almost right word and the right word is the difference between the lightning bug and the lightning."
—Mark Twain

W
W

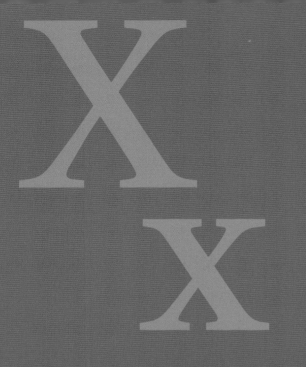

X x

Writing lets us arrange our words so we can share a thought, a feeling, or an observation. When we successfully express ourselves, what once lived inside of us suddenly shines in the light of day.

Sometimes writers express themselves so well their particular words and arrangements become a part of our everyday language.

In *Through the Looking Glass*, Lewis Carroll titled his nonsense poem "Jabberwocky." Now we use the title as a noun, meaning *gibberish*, or an adjective, meaning *senseless*.

The world's longest senseless word sung by children to express approval, *supercalifragilisticexpialidocious*, never appeared in any of P.L. Travers' Mary Poppins books. Walt Disney Studio songwriters created the word especially for the movie.

Some writers borrow expressions to use as pen names, names under which they write. Samuel L. Clemens found the perfect writer's name in the phrase Mississippi River boatmen shouted when the water depth was 12 feet deep and safe—"Mark Twain!"

"Make sure the writing's got your own natural funk all over it."

—Christopher Paul Curtis

X is for eXpression—
well-ordered words held dear,
that best reveal
what one might feel
or see or think or hear.

yellow-haired
he devoured his
warm dinner,
r noticing the
of tomato no
in his bea

l wiz

like t

soup

Everyone has a story to tell—a life story of sorts.

The word *story* comes from the word *history*, which means a narrative of events. And *history's* story? It comes from the Greek word *historia* which means to ask or inquire, to learn and know.

Writing helps you learn and know the story behind your story—the *who, what, when, where, how,* and *why* of you. In *your* story, you claim the screen, you plan your actions, you falter yet somehow succeed. *Your* story recounts the events of *your* life. "Yes!" you'll say, as you write to the end. "That's just how it is!"

Your story is worth telling, but only you can tell it. You choose the words. You wave the wand. You make the magic.

Of course, the magic isn't yours alone. Poet Janet Wong reminds young writers, "No one else can say what you have seen and heard and felt today. But if you tell us well, very well, your stories will seem like our own."

"Yes!" we'll say. "That's just how it is!"

Y y

Y is for Your Story,
yours to live and grow,
of all you do,
and where you've been
and where you hope to go.

Zorro's Robin Hood-like story grabbed readers' hearts when Johnston McCulley told it in 1919. Who could resist the tale of the masked California highwayman, Don Diego Vega, who hid his identity in order to right wrongs? His departing signature told the world he'd been there: three quick sword-drawn lines that formed the letter Z.

How might you sign your name someday beneath *your* story's words to show the world *your* presence? Boldly, in cursive letters, like John Hancock did when he signed the Declaration of Independence? Or with an original mark that shows your spirit?

Perhaps beneath your name you'll place a signature quote that tells the world something about you, the way the authors' quotes throughout this book tell something about writing. Maybe, "I think I can, I think I can, I think I can," from *The Little Engine That Could*. Or Milo's remark from *The Phantom Toll Booth*, "So many things are possible just as long as you don't know they're impossible."

"My advice for children who want to write is, you can start right now."
—Richard Peck

Z? It's for masked Zorro.
His Z-signed tales brought fame.
All knew his mark—
three sword-drawn lines,
though few knew his true name.

P.S.

P.S. is an abbreviation for the Latin phrase "*post scriptum*" which means "after writing." A postscript appears as a word, sentence, or paragraph beneath the letter writer's or author's signature, adding to the previous content.

- The letter *e* is the most frequently used alphabet letter. *The* is the most common word used in English texts.

- English bookseller John Newbery published children's literature in the mid-1700s, including *The History of Little Goody Two-Shoes* in 1765, which many consider the first novel written for children. The American Library Association's annual medal for the most distinguished contribution to American literature for children bears John Newbery's name.

- Home-schooled author Christopher Paolini began writing his first novel *Eragon*, a mix of fantasy and science fiction, at age 15. His parents published the novel privately when he was 19.

- The Library of Congress appointed Jon Scieszka to serve as our country's first National Ambassador for Young People's Literature.

- Magazine publisher Hugo Gernsback created the genre description "science fiction." His magazine *Amazing Stories* published stories by H. G. Wells and Jules Verne. The Hugo Award for Science Fiction Achievement honors him.